The Clearing Barrel

Anthony Roberts

The Clearing Barrel
Copyright ©2021 Anthony Roberts www.Varangiwriting.com
Artwork by Rebecca Roberts
Author Photo by LaRoche Photography

ISBN- 978-1-7333822-7-4

Published by:

Blue Jade Press, LLC

Blue Jade Press, LLC
Vineland, NJ 08360
www.bluejadepress.com

The poem, CPT Ahad previously appeared in Southerly Literary Journal in the Autumn 2016 "Persian Passages" issue

Acknowledgements

If you're reading this, I'm surprised as I rarely read this in other books. The author usually names people and places I don't know. The fact is though, that there are a lot of people to thank. First and foremost is the late Theodore Clymer author of the books "A Duck is a Duck" and "Helicopters and Gingerbread." These were the first books I read on my own and launched me on the course through stacks and shelves that has landed me here.

Next are all of the librarians of the Enoch Pratt Library System in Baltimore, Maryland. All of those annoying questions and strange book requests made by a precocious child have resulted in this book.

A few teachers, Colette Crandall, Ben Feldman, Bob Carusi, Deborah Jagoda, and LTC(ret) Alton Parker, had you not taken the time that you did, I would more than likely be a statistic and not an author.

Three people who know exactly how much they are responsible for my being here. Hank Hilton, Wendy Schwartz, and Elizabeth Manner.

Those in the rooms whose constant example renews daily the gift of sobriety. They are identified by their initials to preserve their anonymity. BP, TD (the Grandsponsor), RH, CA, RD (the Fairy Godsponsor), CJ, CK, DP, CC, GA, XF, AF, JW, KK, JT, FK, thank you.

The Tribe. Those who serve in and out of uniform and with whom I have had the privilege of working alongside in defense of a Nation, yours is the sacrifice few see and fewer understand. When I first started publishing, I was reticent to share that part of myself unsure of how it would be received. I was foolish in that regard; you all have been amazing in your support and encouragement.

The Writers, Poets, Musicians, Artists, and Fellow Story Tellers who encourage, critique, and support, as we all strive to do justice to the things we wish to make real: The late Roger Humes and Sheema Kalbasi who were there at the beginning and published me for the first time, Krista Bremer of the Sun Magazine and her husband Ismail Suayah who have always provided perspective, spirited debate, and friendship, Hexenrauch Quintan Ana Wikswo who saw something in my writing and in me worth sharing with others, Hettie Jones whose presence as living history reminds me of what I aspire to be, Ryan Torres, John McKenna, Malachy McCourt, Larry Kirwan, Damian Voerg, Maria Deasy, Brendan Costello, Shannon Haire, Timothy Liu, Laurie Sheck, Elaine Equi, Shelley Jackson, Mark Bibbins, and so many others who have offered mentorship, encouragement, critique, and friendship, thank you.

To the Beta readers who provided me the one thing I most needed, near immediate feedback: Jackson Hern, Katie Kelaidis, Mark Larson, Annmarie Lockhart, Patrick Moore, Ariana Keshishian, Vince Tirri, and Leslie Gray Streeter, thank you.

To Rebecca Roberts (no relation), who provided the cover art and other art you see in the book. Having another veteran add their perspective through a visual medium only adds to the strength of this work, thank you.

To my editor and publisher Rebecca Bonham who took a mass of poems from me twice and made two books a reality, thank you. Any errors the reader may find in the work are mine, not hers.

Finally, to my family, my wife Dana, and my children Elizabeth, Gianna, Alex and Tristan. You have both celebrated and endured much of what is written about here and then had to put up with me as I balanced work and book and life, giving me the time, I needed to meet deadlines or take a nap. I pray this book is worth your sacrifice.

Foreword

Writers say a lot of things intended to make them sound smart. They use words chosen specifically to sail over the heads of their readers, as if alienating those you propose to reach is a badge of honor. Spoiler alert: It's not. It's alienating. I mean, you're entitled to write for whatever audience you choose, and if that's like three people in an echo chamber who just keep telling you you're brilliant, then so be it. I don't want to read it, but you do.

Anthony Roberts, on the other hand, is one of the smartest people I know. And I'm not just saying that because he asked me to write the foreword for his beautiful collection of poems. It's true. I've met few people who can get to the point of a thing more quickly and succinctly as him, with just the right words and the right amount of humor. Don't take my word for it - read his. What follows is an eloquent love letter to life - to memory and regret, to family and familiarity, to adventure and longing. You can see the form stone on the Baltimore row homes, feel the Old Bay stinging in your paper cuts as the crabs are cracked. Everything he writes about, all the pictures he creates, invites the reader to surrender to it.

What he's done is write a memoir in rhythm. He's told his story in stanzas, in gorgeous tumbling phrases and vulnerable verses that might inspire the reader to delve into their own memories and find the poetry there. I'm so excited for you to turn this page and dive in.

Leslie Gray Streeter
Author, Mother, Journalist, Bestselling Author of
Black Widow: A Sad-Funny Journey Through Grief for People Who Normally Avoid Books With Words Like 'Journey' in the Title

Introduction

"YOU'RE a poet?" The number of times I have heard that as either a statement or a question cannot be calculated. This book answers that question in a way that even its predecessor, Pigtown, did not. Yes, I am a poet. Whether I am a good one is a matter of opinion, but that's not my concern. I am a poet. I ignored that aspect of myself for a while, not realizing that it was necessary to being whole. I started writing again following a deployment to Afghanistan and then decided to put some of the Post 9-11 GI Bill to work pursuing an MFA. That experience gave me both confidence and humility. Both have gone a great way toward making me a better human and that's the goal after all.

That brings us to this book, there are a few things of which I'd like to make you aware. Readers familiar with the earlier work, "Pigtown", understand the autobiographical nature of much of my work. This book has some of that, but I have also looked outward, particularly when it comes to Afghanistan. One person, one perspective, one voice, cannot embody a war, let alone a war now entering its twentieth year. Some of these poems have been influenced by or are an attempt to give voice to the perspectives of others, I appreciate their trust with their stories and I hope I've done them justice.

So, let's wrap this up if you're still reading. Go read some poetry. Then go live. Eat good food, drink good wine, good beer, or good coffee. Call (don't text) a friend. Get on a train and go somewhere you haven't been before. Hit the gym and go for a new PR. Hit the range and try therapy in different calibers. Talk to someone who doesn't look or think like you. Volunteer at an animal shelter. Listen to live music, listen to any music. Go to a bookstore or a library! Just live.

Yes, I am a poet, and I am grateful to you the reader for finding my words worthy of your time and attention.

Anthony Roberts
Alexandria, NJ
November, 2020

Dedicated to the memory of Mary Theresa Roberts. The first poems I heard were spoken in your voice, but I still don't know why you liked Rod McKuen so much. You knew the first book was coming but didn't live to see it. The best I can do is dedicate this one to you.
Thank you, Mom.

Table of Contents

When?

When irony loses its appeal and you decide to forego
the cynical sestina or the structurally perfect sonnet of a
Shakespeare in SoHo...

When you are ready to trade in the written equivalent of
a Prius or a Subaru for the more defined lines of an old
Volvo or a used BMW

When you decide to skip the reading in the comfortable
knowledge that
what you will hear
is what you heard last month
from the same voices
with different adjectives

When the phrase "open mic "carries with it the same
dread as the words "inoperable, stage four, terminal"

When you leave behind the need for ego feeding
by your presence at someone else's reading

When you're ready to close your eyes to the world
rather than condemn

Then, it is time to write

I. Maps of the Mind

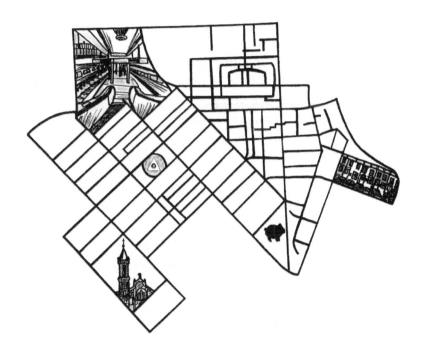

Grandfather

100 years ago
the Spanish flu was passing through a world that still
smelled of the rotted corpses of the Great War

The Angel that had passed over Egypt stood next to its
descendant the Black Plague
both looked on in admiration

Grandfather was an infant
swaddled in superstition and prayer
after the death of a generation at the hands of Maxim,
Vickers, and Browning, what was the death of a child
other than a minor inconvenience

But he grew to thrive and helped his parents survive the
inconvenience of his brothers passing
St. Gerald of Baltimore canonized in the mind and eyes
of all who knew him

No doubt now singing sweetly with the angelic choirs
because that is what you're supposed to do when you
die as a child
His name could be invoked alongside Saints Joseph and
Patrick for intercession

Or in the nights of solitary regression
could be sobbed into the pillow of the brother who
always missed him

The brother's ghost walked beside grandfather
up Carroll Street
down Ostend
to Hamburg
to the Church where he prayed every day

light a candle for Gerald
kneel beside mom Virginia and father Frank

Grandfather James
the key to the call box
shiny silver and retired on his belt
the mark of respectability among the Irish
to be a retired cop
to have authority in the new world
denied in the old
a land where self determination
was ruled Fenian terrorism
in America, it was simply trading the shillelagh for a
  billy club

Grandfather as child heard
Jim's hard brogue of Tyrone wrapping itself around the
sounds of the Hail Mary
a rosary a day for Gerald in heaven
a rosary a day for life during the depression
a rosary a day lights the way along the path of
  redemption

A rosary wrapped around the hard scarred knuckles of a
  beat cop
a rosary that keeps going decade after decade becomes
impossible to stop
the beads change the prayers remain
the hands around them age the prayers stay the same

Grandfather becomes of age
and finds himself enchanted
by the Greek girl whose parents own the restaurant
around the corner

The story of the courtship is known only to he and she
they started to keep secrets from the rest of the world
even then
and a new war rages on other shores
until December
when ships were aligned so bombers couldn't miss
he is married on Christmas Day

His son's screaming entry into the world is heard from
  a distance
over the din of North Africa and Italy
as other fathers prepare to die in Normandy
grandfather out west amidst the desert cracked bruised
and sterile
trains to land on ocean sands
and put an end to the yellow peril

What would have been an inevitable death outside of
  Tokyo
was postponed by the end of the war
Grandfather headed east with the war behind him and a
mushroom cloud looking over his shoulder

The new America was one of confusion for grandfather
his son in the arms of his in-laws
his wife still really a war bride
and the reality of life now unavoidable
there was no hope of dying in battle anymore

Grandfather set to work
and two more sons followed
in the heyday of the gold standard
and the new standard of living
there was a TV
and now the drive to the Church
where he knelt alongside his mother and father

Jim now consigned to earth from which the priest said
he came
walking a beat in heaven
with Gerald holding his hand

America of the fifties and sixties
Grandfather was breathing in the golden age
and with it the asbestos sands
that turned his body into an hourglass that no one could
 see
the tick of a watch winding down
that had fallen into the couch
you could hear it but you didn't know what it was

Somewhere in the sixties
Grandfather felt left behind
and Grandmother claimed her own mind
hiding a book on the back of the shelf
Our Bodies, Ourselves
and he was baffled by the home that turned against him
sons always spoiled now rebelled
told him to go to hell
each one taking a different path and gone
Grandfather David mourned his Absaloms and prayed
for their return

And they did
with wives and children
marrying in reverse order
youngest to oldest
the wives of the sons
dutifully pregnant
carrying the progeny to replace the loss of the previous
generation
Virginia and Frank joined Jim and Gerald

Their names now the intentions of the Christmas Eve
Mass in the Church which their patrimony had built
all that remained of them in the world
were their names dutifully inscribed
on a book that rested on the altar
that they had prayed in front of for decades

Grandfather came into his own with grandchildren
his sons struggled with their failings
families splintered and shattered
the shards of the picture frame that had fallen from the
  wall
so he and grandmother stepped
In to fill the voids
material
spiritual
emotional

While the sons struggled
without and within
atoning for a myriad of sins
and the wives/mothers weaved in out and about

Grandfather shielded his grandchildren as best he could
taking them to the same place that gave him solace
taught them to kneel and pray before the same altar
he'd known as a child
they knelt beside ghosts
Jim
Virginia
Frank
Gerald
ghosts who interceded for them

As storms passed
new ones formed
Grandfather and Grandmother
the safe harbor
and the house with the brick front porch
and the green painted planks in back
covered by the metal awning
became the lighthouse
where the children found shelter
from the wind, rocks, and shoals
sometimes the wind found its way in
Grandfather would cough
and no one noticed

Waiting in Penn Station

An Amtrak train
heading south
as I head east
I hear "Baltimore"
I remember
Baltimore Penn Station
my injection site
into the arteries of America

My first train ride alone
April of 1990
seated on polished wooden oak benches
unchanged since the 40s

"I took the train from here to basic training"
my grandfather's ghost reminds me of the conversation
that day
I didn't know he was dying
what it took him to drive me there
I was a selfish child
ready to begin my own journey
-his ghost speaks-

"I know you value it more now than then, but it made
me happy to see you journeying on your own. It made
me happy to see you already seeking freedom."

He's been dead 30 years
finally, I understand
why he loved trains
they gave him freedom too

Amtrak
Amtrak the carrier
of me the human virus
America my host
viruses evolve
to defeat the vaccines
that seek their destruction
there is a vaccine for me and those like me
it is called poverty
it was designed to keep me in place
I mutated before they had time to make a new one

And I traveled throughout my host
Kentucky
Massachusetts
Connecticut
Pennsylvania
New York
North Carolina
South Carolina
Florida
California

Changing into a more virulent form
countering every vaccine
until today
waiting in Penn Station
with coffee in hand

I hear my grandfather's last words on earth to me
"I want you to be happy. That will make me proud"
he rode next to me on the train today

Crab Feast

A red crab painted on a white board
The people lined up around the block and Old Bay
  burns your nose
Bushel baskets with steam rising put into the back of a
  van

Visions of cracked claws and shells, lung, mustard, and
"don't eat that!", staining, soaking through newspaper

Jim Palmer's face turns orange then tears, Earl Weaver
is still smiling

Wooden mallets stained rust and brown beat a staccato
rhythm cracking through to the meat within

"The claw meat is the best", says Uncle Don
"Back fin is the best" says Aunt Mary
"What do you know about crabs, you're from
Pennsylvania!"
This argument brought to you by 30 years of Marriage
and National Premium Dark, the official beer of
Pigtown

Cigarette smoke hangs thick in the church hall
giving texture to coarse conversations
The fat fingered priest says fuck a lot
crab meat trapped beneath bitten nails
that caress a Salem 100 like the Blessed Sacrament

Through a small window in a steel door, it looks like a
kaleidoscope or a snow globe in the hands of a drunk
Hovering in that place forever

By now every adult in that room is dead

Ornaments of Baltimore Empire

Marble steps stand beckoning
before small interconnected villas

They are the bases of pillars
that lead to the temples
of working class aspirations

Father enters through the portico
the entryway floor
a mosaic of small glass and stone tiles

A day at the factory complete
a small smile as the hand traces the plaster wall

Roma Victa

Through the house the sounds
of domestic bliss
a television
a radio
2 children
all competing for attention
Mother in the background
but in control of it all
even Father
especially Father

To learn the value of money
and humility
the pride of ownership
the children join their mothers
on warm sunny days
buckets of Ajax
hard bristle brushes

Steps scrubbed
to a shine so bright
that a statue of Venus
could be placed upon them

Sun sets-moonlight
against the white
the sight of the bright
pillars that light
the streets at night
all roads lead to Home

Roma Victa

Preakness 1995

Did you know that the Preakness after you
I won $500
by picking a horse whose name I liked:
Timber Country
paid 6 to 1
I also made $200 in tips that day at work
walked out at 7pm with $700 in my pocket

I bought a bottle of Bushmills
a bottle of Veuve Cliquot
went to a friend's house warming party
drank the champagne off of the breasts of a red head
her name was Colette
she is of no consequence
other than being a bubbly footnote

She was a nice girl
she liked who she thought I was
But she grew tired of me
When she found she could only get so far
before she hit a wall
that had your name spray painted all over it
she wanted to be loved
wanted to hear me say it to her

She said it to me
every time I was inside her
and I chose those moments
to change positions
so she'd forget I didn't respond
but eventually she figured it out
the bed was only so big
she was only so flexible
and I was only so distracting

So a couple of months after the Preakness
when the saddle blanket of Black Eyed Susan's was
    wilted and dead
and Timber Country was put out to stud or the glue
    factory
She stopped taking my calls

She wanted to be loved
but unlike me
she picked the wrong horse

What if?

I am the one you love in memory
I am the "what if" you think of
when the kids are in school
and you are at work
at home
rushing between soccer games

You remember the places of our youth
how I walked beside you without fear
because the only thing I was afraid of
was you walking beside me
and my giving away in word or appearance
how I felt about you

You remember with guilt
those times you heard about me later
secure in your stability
my own wanderlust
my obscurity
a validation of your choosing the straight path
telling your friends
"thank God I dumped him when I did"

You learned of my madness in some country or other
my lack of direction
my veering from
idea to idea
passion to passion
person to person
place to place
And found solace in your little home
in its secure space
and the role you cut to fit you

It hugged your curves
and the breasts swollen with mother's milk
versus my threadbare coat of a traveler
that even a gypsy would be ashamed to wear

Until now
when all of the memory
all of the madness
all of the moments
of my wandering
are made into the shaped
and bound testament
of a confession put to poetry

You look around at the empty house
children grown and gone
your prince now a king
no longer strong
no longer bold
on the throne you gave him
revealed to be brass
instead of gold

Your dress hangs where it should cling
and clings where it should hang
you have become a broodmare
I remain a mustang

So ask "what if" as you wish
ask "what might have been"
if you had viewed me for what I was
rather than an unforgivable sin

26 August 2017

I'm not ready to bury my mother
To return her to the earth
To see the past sealed up by the vaults concrete lid

I'll remember her hands the most

Hands that I felt swing me through the air
Guide me tying my shoes
Slapped my mouth for profanity
Sewed my favorite blanket
Embroidered a family tree

Held up in defense as a drunken rage made her its target
Held countless patients hands as they grasped for life
Held me when I wept at loss
Held me when we wept together

Hands that became bent and twisted as the disease ran
its course until they resembled tree roots

Hands that in death will hold a rosary
and will no longer send their message of constant pain

The pain will be in my hands after carrying her for the
  last time
After gently setting her coffin down
The way she laid me in bed when I'd fallen asleep

I'll fall asleep again one-day mother
and I pray it will be you who wakes me
I don't want to see Saints or Savior
I want my mom to wake me up from the nightmare of
  her passing

Eulogistic Reflection

Two years of waxen recall
and the reminder of the overly floral smell that inhabits
  all funeral parlors

Rather than myrrh we use roses, orchids, and lilies to
mask the formaldehyde scent of paused decomposition

We pretend around the coffin
that the deceased is simply sleeping.
Our voices lower in tone as we approach the casket
a murmur about appearance before the uncaring
  occupant
the lie that the dead look so natural where they lay

Do we whisper in front of the husk of snake scale? The
shell of a cicada? The conch vacated by a hermit crab?

Speaking fondly of the dead in the off chance that we
might be named in the inheritance.
We call this respect
lying to ourselves in life about death

Embalmed pinned
waxed shaped
fixed in place
we still fear the dead
and our secrets that they took with them
or perhaps that they now know.

Before mahogany polished
into glowing majestic glory
so radiant
you'd think it was the vehicle
by which the deceased entered the kingdom

The evolution of the coffin
from sublime wood to mystical metal
available for cremation as a rental

The wealthy demanded more than a pine box since it
had no locks
to keep the past from rising and reclaiming what the
present didn't earn

Today I smelled orchids in a stuffy room
and I wept

Tchotchkes

A child breaks a favorite knickknack
and rushes to glue to it together
both to escape punishment
and from a profound sense of remorse
having changed the world
of the mother they love
and the mother
first to anger
and then
seeing the child's pain
is moved within
reminded of what it is
to be a child
in a world of breakable things
and the haphazardly glued together object
remains on display
until it is simply part of the scenery

one day

the child now a mother
finds the piece again
sees it through
a mother's eyes
smiles
cries
Remembers

It's the broken things that we put back together that
bind us when we're gone

Prime

Three parts of a prime number
accompanied by
a distorted view
through a photographed facsimile
that comes to 43

Part I
underway at another prime
13
when poems entered the mind
Morrison lamenting his cock
sore and crucified
15 years dead by then
he didn't rise again
I had to pull the words up
from the page
wordsonwordsonwords
in madcap run on adolescence

Part II
followed out of the grand exit
Snake Pliskin saved the president
I just had to save myself
Baltimore remains far more deadly than
even New York
I used red clay, scrub pine, and a blue cord
to slough off a body of dead skin
and found a discipline that remains...
something resented but essential

Part III
was an unexpected plot twist
compartmentalizing
it was easier to hide that way
learning to lie from another prime (7)
creates Tupperware for the soul
vacuum sealed for freshness
so that when you open the container
it hurts just as much

Rather than Tupperware
I'd rather have a Mr. Clean Magic Eraser
and undo an entire past
drawing a new one thanks to a 64 box of crayons
with the sharpener in the back so as to avoid blurred
   lines
all the parts pressed together
like the thighs of a middle aged stripper
bits of crayon melted together
makes me wonder
why did Crayola do away with Prussian Blue?

Passing Through

The child confronts death by railing at an unfair god
the child is the center of its own universe
when you take love away the gravity is lost
the universe tears itself into a tightly wound ball

The adult holding all of that in confronts death by
releasing that love
a new universe is created from the old
with an understanding of the passing of things God is
perhaps forgiven
perhaps ignored perhaps forgotten
galaxies turn
suns burn
planets thrive
driven by the why

The aged one with nothing left to hold confronts death
with a smile
the universe is one of galaxies long dead
on the other side of that universe is a place where
Hawking and Einstein no longer matter
where Aquinas and Dawkins are both right
where there are no rules that make sense
where there is no sense to make rules of divine comedic
chaos

On the other side of nothing is laughter
Jesus wept
and weeps
and will do so again
for each of my repeated sins
absolution gained and lost
attained and squandered
through each new city I wandered

Wondering at the mystery contained within
the bars and restaurants where I could begin
to shape and form the poet I wanted to be
to shape and form the person I wanted you to see
until the inevitable rejection
that I wrote off to how
you perceived my reflection

I wanted to be a saint
I wanted to be an apostle
preaching to the masses my own gospel
the world was converted
my best efforts subverted
by the prophet I found in a bottle

Voce Profundo

I. Ecco l'Uomo
The indictment of the state of being
which states that we are made in the image of God
deliberately flawed or
a false narrative in order to give hope
to the poor bastard who never had a chance
who in a world more kind would have been left on the
  mountain
to starve mouth agape suckling the sky
for lack of knowledge of a breast
until blessed death consumes the child
sparing him from the lessons of failure that last a
  lifetime
instead failing only once before gaining his reward

The conviction of the state of being
where the weak become self-aware
achieving furious resentment hating their ersatz
  superiors
for the sale of a lottery ticket that lost
leaving them to flail about in unenlightened servitude
having learned just enough to eat, drink, and copulate
without the foresight of understanding
without the capability to dream

II. Ecco il Mondo
The condemnation of the state of being
that results in the beating that leaves no marks
save for the wrinkles and shriveled skin around a body
that labors for a mind not up to the task of survival
enabled by a vicious kindness
that confuses enslavement with entitlement
dependence with development
their teachers lied with lessened lessons

of equality and egalitarian egotism
truncated truths easier to teach
than the tallied torments that must be endured

The execution of the state of being
voices demanding
Let all things end in judgment
Let God as he knows himself
be judged
by humanity
for humanity
for the crime against humanity
which commits crimes against humanity
believing that it is made in god's image
not knowing that God works in the dark
and has never once looked in the mirror

Proof of Being a Gen-X Poet

We had our brief flirtation with David Foster Wallace
who left us essays
before he left us
a dangling participle

Proof now comes
in more morbid ways
particularly in the form of obituaries

Adrienne Rich
Phillip Levine
Linda Gregg
Leonard Cohen
Seamus Haney

These are but five of the voices
who put us onto the path of being poets

When we started writing they were more alive than we
we followed with pens and notebooks
ears attuned for the sounds of nuance and glottal stops

Their voices faded and we found our own
and forgot the debt we owed
for we were as alive as they
until they stopped being alive

Today
reading Linda Gregg's obituary
The New York Times told me
I have reached the limit
of my 5 free articles for the month it took me a moment
to remember what 5 people had died

?

The most dangerous form of punctuation is the question mark.

Its sole purpose is to lead to an answer.
Answers sometimes are not what you want to hear

Perhaps that's why Socrates replied to questions with questions of his own.
better to let the student
come to the answer himself
and be his own source of enlightenment
or disappointment.

The question mark carries with it the ability to change a life irrevocably.
Did the Doctor call?
What happened?
Where were you?
Have you been drinking?
Who is he?
Who is she?
Are you telling the truth?
Can we talk?

There will be a question mark in my epitaph.
Once the funeral is over and I'm left alone,
those who pass by will have cause to laugh
as they read the words on my stone

"Is that all?"

Holy Fool

I have no wisdom
only broken pieces of glass that look like diamonds
when you hold them under a streetlight

They cut into flesh in a halogen glow
prismatic stigmata of a crimson rainbow that never
ceases to flow rivulet stream that claims to redeem and
soaks through still another brown paper bag holding
Popov Vodka

I am Dostoevsky's fool, a drunken messiah, a castaway
ordained with sweat, grime, and the smell of a body that
has not showered in days

The odious body draped with unwashed clothes, makes
for the юродивый, a coronation robe for my clothing
they want not

The balm and oil that poured over David's head
clogged his ears and he did not hear what Samuel said
hearing an echo of battle Uriah's death rattle while
Bathesheba shared his bed

So he said
So he said

To ease your conscience
you give me ten dollars tonight there will be a
celebration in the kingdom ensuring I am numb and
free from mourning a mother's dead son.

I no longer write psalms with the glass embedded in my
palms.

A (Text) Message to Garcia

I delete the text messages
that contain
bad news
or criticisms
or complaints
or goodbyes
their disappearance
puts them out of my mind
it brings peace I find
so that I can pretend
until I see the name again
that they never happened

I throw away the letters
that contain
well I don't know what they contain
since I ensure they remain
unopened
the message to Garcia made its way to me
but which Garcia did the sender mean?
Ricardo?
Paulo?
Israel?
Jerry?
I know too many Garcias
to worry about
which one the sender meant
I hope they don't mind
I gave it to the first one I could find
Tomas Garcia
of Elizabeth, NJ
who received a message
from Ed McMahon's ghost
that he may already be a winner

When I last spoke to Tomas
no one had arrived
with a check to take away his pain
but he was given comfort by
the subscriptions he'd purchased
to Cosmo and Vogue

He texted me last night
bemoaning his lot in life
I read the message
and deleted it

I tell myself it didn't happen

A Diner in North Carolina

Her drawl is as thick as the gravy on the plate. Her skin
as pale as the fired clay upon where breakfast sits.

In the south, the biography is served with the meal. The
portion is generous. Served with a smile where the lips
move up and the eyes remain dead

Crow's feet wrap around eyes that when younger,
stared upward at chestnut trees. When the nuts were
harvested and roasted they matched her hair before she
started bleaching it.

Her hands red, rough, and cracked, match the drought
afflicted red clay outside, only pine and palmetto grow
here she complains.

She wraps her arms about herself and her hands rub her
shoulders remembering when they were soft and
caressed the shoulders of another.

Her breasts bound tightly within the confines of a bra,
the underwire pokes through the nylon of her blouse;
the illusion of pillowed comfort matched by the hard
biscuits that soak up the gravy like a wheat field after a
storm.

Her hips block the view to the kitchen, parted further
with the birth of each child, each son of Cain now
trying to pry a life from resentful soil.

Silence is taken as solidarity. The eyes soften as the
meal goes on, finishing with a hopeful glance washed
down by coffee.

The invitation for dessert is declined, the tip left on the table a consolation prize. She clears the plates and looks for someone with a bigger appetite.

Road Trip Through the Confederacy

I.
When you start to drive the speed limit
it means that there is no place you want to go
all the places where you stopped and wanted to stay
have disappeared in the rear view mirror behind you

When you start to drive the speed limit
you see on your left those passing by
enroute to possibility or probability
some idea or vision place and time
where they belong
where they want to be

When you start to drive the speed limit
you start to pay attention
to the side roads
the exit ramps
the names of places
that you won't see
because there isn't time
or you tell yourself
another time

When you start to drive the speed limit
the radio plays even worse songs than usual
and you find yourself listening to NPR
and Terri Gross' voice finds you in

Norfolk
Salisbury
Easton
Milford
Dover
Newark

Wilmington
Philadelphia
Trenton

It follows you north
the soft tones
of an interview from 10 years ago
with someone who died yesterday
why didn't you listen back then?

Because you thought you had more time
So did they
So you drive the speed limit
with nowhere to go
getting better gas mileage
with a dead man's dry chuckle at a bad joke
filling your ears
on I-95N

II.
Virginia
When you start to drive the speed limit
leaving Ghent
driving near MLK
the Hasidim unloading the trunk of his Camry
looks at you wearily
even with white skin to him
you're a foreigner
and you pass the places
of the men with green faces
Dam Neck
Little Creek
and hear the sounds of tridents
impaling Virginia girls

Onto the bridge tunnel
bridge tunnel
bridge
7 miles of contemplation
with a bay surrounding you
alone with thoughts
fear of drowning
and the fear that maybe
you're already dead
and only your body is driving home
when you cross onto solid ground
there is a stainless steel light pole
where someone has spray painted
"Croatan"

Onward northward
following the route of hope
and smoked hams and jams
all for sale by the roadside
with pies particularly pecan
though I've not see a tree
here in this marshland
where the air smells of salt
and brackish humidity tells
of an ocean somewhere
to the right

You'll be home by tonight
as you see the stars and bars
a painted reminder
that you are leaving a defeated nation
that mourns a myth of its own creation

III.
Maryland
When you start to drive the speed limit
you find yourself
on ancestral land
granted to your family
centuries ago
but you feel no connection to this place
the tobacco plantations
are as dead as the slaves who tended them
they have given way
to strip malls
and the dual irons of poverty and geography
that create colorblind enslavement
and the overseer's 4th great-granddaughter
and the slave's fourth great-grandson
slave away together
behind the counter of the gas station

Hit Me

Poems composed in bathtubs
hold more meaning
writing during baptism
at least your body is clean
if not your mind or soul
and what of the mind and soul
you eventually lose one
and the other becomes
a bargaining chip
in a game of blackjack
with a God
who looks like Penn Gillette

Carvel

What's the crunchy chocolate stuff in the ice cream
  cake
little bits of broken childhood
memories of blowing out the candles
in a room already filled with cigarette smoke
the daredevil years

When adults weren't looking
dripping hot wax on the skin
thrilling at the burn
that cooled so quickly
peeling back to see skin now pink beneath
as it was when you were born
before there were any candles to blow out

Each one extinguished a reminder
that your own light is dimming
until you lay there
seeing that last candle flickering above you
before everything goes dark
and you strain to share the final words
that those who love you must hear from you

Fucking Cookiepuss

Love and Baklava
(Lessons from a Greek Man)

The debate can be made as to what is more fragile
sheets of phyllo or the human heart

The heart
thick muscle
that drives the body for its entire life
charged with current
pulsing lifeblood through vessels it cannot see
knowing time only by blood's movement through
ventricles and return

When broken the heart does not heal
only grows scar tissue
that holds the muscle together
tomorrow becomes the goal
tomorrow and perhaps they'll find a way to again make
the heart whole

Labor without pleasure each pulsing measure
working toward the inevitable she' ma and shalom
God and death waltzing to scarred metronome
the tides of a lifespan marked by the beach that erodes
with each year
until skin is stretched taut and thin

Phyllo is more easily repaired
sheet laid flat
if torn
gently pinched between the fingers of Yaya and pressed
  smooth
the fissure no longer present
butter brushed over to seal
vulnerable thin membrane

Strengthened by layer on layer
sheet
butter
brush
sheet
butter
brush
sheet
butter
brush
Repeat

Until the dough becomes strong enough to withstand
pressure of pecan, pistachio, and walnuts
heat of a three hundred and twenty-five-degree oven
for an hour and fifteen minutes

The searing sweetened syrup already prepared
rosewater, honey, lemon, sugar
balm or anointing oil
poured over still hot dough
now hardened by its infernal ordeal
you hear it sizzle as it seeps into the spaces between
dough and filling

A protective barrier the heart lacks
sugary scar tissue that encases all
leaving behind a smile
and the flutter of a scarred heart
when it is consumed
by one who knows
how much it hurt to make it

Great Grandfather

The Greek sailor
whose wanderlust and blood
are my inheritance
found his way to a place
where he was landlocked
lovelocked
stereotyped

He owned restaurants
he gave his grandsons houses
by the time his great-grandson arrived
he had little left to give me
save for memories
they have lasted longer than the houses

It was his gift that became my sentence
it was his gift that unlocked my prison
Greek myths are replete with stories like these
where the gods reward
then punish
then reward
if man can endure the punishment

Sitting in a high chair in his kitchen
then a booster seat
watching grape leaves from the yard
turned into Dolmas
that I chewed happily
he used Concord grape leaves
and cursed a place
too cold to grow olives

Cursed many things
so much so
that my first words
were the profanities
I learned from him

I was too young
to join him at the stove
or the oven
content and confined
a spectator to creation
but I watched
later my grandmother would observe
that my hands moved like his when cooking
the turn of the wrist with the spatula
the whole arm shaking spices
my hands moved like his when cooking
they still do

The punishment came
with the house given to the grandson
a neighborhood
with boundaries determined
by salary and status
you could go beyond the borders
but you must always return
that was the rule
unspoken
understood
unbroken
generations of families
separated by maybe a couple of houses
or a street
sometimes separated
by only a floor

The punishment was the gift
a home
with borders
the challenge was to endure
evolve
escape
A test
the same test he had passed as a boy
making the journey between Chios and Thessaloniki
until he gained the strength
to move across the ocean
the grandsons had failed the test
they all returned
receiving a home
as a consolation prize

It was time to test me
then he died
he left behind a key
stacks of magazines
that took up an entire closet
that were willed to me
National Geographic
a child of 7
with the world piled in front of him

So in 1980
I went through the piles
and found the April 1976 issue
with a map of the Soviet Union and its peoples
words foreign but familiar places
that he had spoken of
presented themselves to me

Moscow
Leningrad
Kharkov
Vilnius
Odessa
(his ghost talked about the port of Odessa with
fondness)
Volgograd
Tbilisi
Klaipeda
Polanka
Slav
Tatar
Cossack
Uzbek
Tajik
Ukrainian
Chechen
Georgian
Armenian

In many issues
more maps
each with its own path
that led
out of room
out of the house
out of the neighborhood
out of the city
toward the sea

Now in a kitchen the size of the first floor of that house
I eat dolmas
my hands mimic his at the stove
I see the land outside
soil fertile

Fertile enough
to grow grapes
I'll have my own leaves
and I'll curse a climate too cold for olives
and give my children maps

Chios

I dream of the Aegean
and the blue around Chios
lamb seasoned dripping on pita
a block of feta
blue black olives shine
against the ivory of a table cloth
and the bright white of the sun
that doesn't burn

The Ouzo untouched a reminder
of the damnation of the Irish genes
pass by
pass by
until the taste of the olive drowns out the scent of anise

Sent away across the blue
to the brown of a foreign harbor
where a young man
started on a path
that a century later finds me here
trying to find the words to say
that I want to go home
in a language I don't know

Arrival

Sailing closer to where things began
the gray shape of the island in the distance
begins to become more defined
white homes on hillsides
against the blue sea I sail
becoming brighter
wind behind me
sun above me

I am closer to home
I see a white house in my mind
you stand in the doorway
seeing my ship approach
you walk down the path on the hill
eyes never leaving me
 standing at the bow
fixed on your man's approach
your hips swaying in the way
that tells me you are happy I have returned
assuring me of the welcome that awaits
when the moon replaces the sun
and we lay in bed
our bodies matching the rhythm
of the waves that brought me home to you

Topography

The Soldier has an appreciation for and understanding
of terrain from years spent learning the language of
land then conversing with it through solitary days and
nights carrying the weight of the ruck filled with his
own thoughts. Put a man in the wilderness and he will
return more man or more animal; it depends on his
sense of self

Moving along the earth calling it by its names: spur,
draw, valley, hill, cut, depression, fill, ridge, line, cliff

Learning how to move to find your point of destination
to determine your own location the beckoning call of
the trees dead reckoning until you see the place you
were meant to be

To determine place to make correction demands
understanding of intersection and resection two
azimuths shot toward known points and there you are

There is a beauty in the map translated to the land and
in places not yet explored the desire to understand I
have seen the map of your body

I want to learn your topography and feel the geography
of your flesh navigating with hands and tongue into the
places I have not seen I want to conquer with all of the
power of empire behind me plant my flag and say I
claim this for my Queen I want to arrive in peace with
all of the humility of a missionary and kneel down
before you and thank god

You take my compass into your hands for you it is
always pointed North

Red Pen

1.
Red ink
denotes
notes
not
no

No
no notes
not notes no
not notes
no

2.
Red ink denotes
reduction of the poem
redaction of words
beneath sanguine condemnation
reaction (negative) to the poem
rejection
reflection leads to
recollection
of the memoryideathing
that resulted in the poem
followed by revision
that leads to
something lost in the
original meaning

This is called editing

3.
Red ink denotes crucifixion
upon literary Calvary
after a night spent
in the Gethsemane of
inspiration
"Father, if it be your will
let this cup pass me by, but thy will be done."

4.
Red ink denotes composition
Son of David hears the poem in his head
Son of a bitch I can't get this
right
write
rite

5.
Red Ink denotes
Wrong
or so the ink tells me
and on the third day
I'll write again
and chase you from the temple
fashioning a whip
from Kenneth Goldsmith's beard
that will then be sold on E-Bay
profit is the epitome of the uncreative act

I can't stand poets
they'd be the first
to offer Judas
10 times as much silver
just to keep Jesus
from making it to the workshop

Semi-Colon

In blue black on her forearm
a reminder of a man who loved her
but hated himself
checking out rather than checking in
checked into a new room somewhere

She smiles when she sees mine

Tells me her story
the irony lost upon her
of scissors, twin blades
honed to gleaming
ever snipping at my neck and throat
her voice punctuating the snips
until they are one and the same
the full bosomed muffin topped oracle
of the strip small salon
shares her wisdom

The idea
of the pause not the period
a way to recognize each other
acknowledging that is glad to see
in the flesh in the flesh
a fellow member of the society
returned like a Lazarus
who without a messiah
had to resurrect himself
you may not smell as good
coming out of the tomb
but at least you don't owe god anything

After the semicolon
a long stream of commas follows
until you reach the period where the story was supposed
to end
and you're laid out beneath a stone
an inverted exclamation point
in a verdant green yard
full of periods

That are supposed to be semicolons
according to that guy who raised Lazarus
but nobody's heard from him in a while

A Child Asleep After A Journey

The child's eyes closed
Asleep after a long trip
The sound of the waves
A soothing metronome

Hair tousled
A smooth face
Free of worry
As all children should be

Let him sleep
Let the sun warm him
Should he grow cold
Cradle him
Against your chest
Safe

His lungs are filled with water

Un Sommeil D'enfant Après un Voyage

Les yeux D'enfant fermés
Endormi après un long voyage
Le bruit des vagues
Un métronome apaisante

cheveux dans le vent
Le visage lisse
Sans souci
Comme tous les enfants devraient être

Laisser lui dormer
Que le soleil lui chauffer
Doit-il se refroidira
Cradle lui
Contre votre poitrine
Sûr

Ses poumons sont remplis d'eau

Bobby Walsh

I loved a girl whose father died
His lungs as black as the coal
that fed his family
filled his pockets
built his house
and killed him at 45

I held that girl when she cried
Even though I, a child of the city
born in a row house
boundaries of life determined by concrete squares
couldn't understand a life
spent living in backbreaking darkness

I forgave that girl when she lied
about her idyllic past
her wealthy family
her big house
because of the shame she felt.
When they brought her daddy out of the trailer to bury
  him
they couldn't clean the coal off his hands

To The Paris Review on the Occasion of Your Rejection

Dear Editor

Too weak to fail alone, so this week I choose you who
has also been thrown over the barrel of life and taken
from behind while you claimed not to mind the signs of
the times my editor demanded that this rhyme lest I be
slammed or worse enjambed I had no idea what that
word meant until I was 40 unwilling to repent with
Cabernet to make me portly a Chesterton for the
damned and there I'll make it enjambed again to meet
the editors demand when the wine ran out there was the
realization that the editor was a figment of my
imagination seen in last night's altercation that ended
with me challenging a midget to a game of miniature
golf there are my nights or at least how I remember
them 20 years later oh the sights of a drunken
September committed in some way to paper I tried to
take flight by whiskey infused member you never see a
middle aged satyr except in the school for the blind
where a blonde statue was once kind enough to let me
kiss her in a manner intemperate but she waived the
requirement of actually being a poet in this way did I
receive my diploma with honors being able to see
though I couldn't read the Braille that raised the letters
to intrude on my reality so I stepped on the diploma
with golf shoes until it made more sense
Write back before the second coming but don't worry
when she remembered you she told me she hadn't
noticed you first.

Hosea

Words and rhythm are dated, archaic, obsolete poetry
just listen to David's psalms tripping over modern
tongues
at the end of the poem
not one stone is left upon the other
the rubble of language
turned to dust not unlike the first temple

Jerusalem, you don't weep
how could you
it's a place you've never known
harps hanging from willows
a people lament
and you tell them to get over it

Hosea in the back room
is wailing at the memory
of how it felt
to love a whore

She asked that her things be returned
arriving without fanfare she loaded her stuff
and disappeared

The things she gave him
like her body
now in the hands of another man
If he could he would burn them all

A prophet in love with a whore
is a man doubly damned
Mocked by Satan, forsaken by God
when all he wants is love

Modern Poetry

The Pranksters Bus read: "Further"
This bus reads: "far enough"
Kesey's ghost shakes his head
and Rochambeaus David Foster Wallace

The tourists aren't pranksters
they are the placenta of creativity
literary critics cum anthropologists
who:
Label
Identify
Analyze
Parse
Place
Dissect
Section
Resection
Compartmentalize

Every soundletterword
every punctuation mark
ensuring a homogenous purity

That will bore the fuck
out of future generations

And your biography had better be interesting
because the editors
will ensure
that your words are not

Your words tossed haphazardly
about this barren Acropolis
like the bones in the colosseum

Where poets who eschewed rules
were fed to the lions.
When devoured, they screamed
in Iambic Pentameter

Duet
(A poem for two voices)

Hope
is a four letter word
is a word that earns derision
is for those who failed to plan
is the last desperate gasp for air
before you slip beneath the waves a third time

-in case you were wondering, if you go into the desert
seeking solitude, god will leave you alone-

Hope
is what a boy carries who didn't study for the test
is what a woman holds when she feels the lump in her
  breast
is what a mother clings to when the baby in the womb
  ceases to kick
is what the addict invokes when he starts to feel sick
is the refuge of the weak

-in case you were wondering, if you go into the desert
seeking solitude, god will leave you alone-

This is what I was taught
this is what I believed
this is the gospel I preached
another heretic who emerged from the desert
like so many others
who confused ordinary solitude
with a divine encounter

-in case you were wondering, if you go into the desert
seeking solitude, god will leave you alone-

I returned
with a message to convert the world
people of what's left of Jerusalem
hear me
I have not found God
love is a hormonal imbalance
life is a sexually transmitted disease
hope is folly
leave your homes
return to Babylon
give up
surrender

The Greeks lied to us all
"Abandon hope all ye who enter here" is not what is
written over the gate as you enter Hades
It is what is written on the other side as you walk back
out into the world of the allegedly living

-in case you were wondering, if you go into the desert
seeking solitude, god will leave you alone-

A Sudden Departure

A poem about footprints
and a god who walks beside you
who carries you while you cry
or words to that effect

Resides in a cracked frame
on the floor, against the wall
above it a bloody handprint
smeared in a downward arc

This was the last will and testament
of the hermit who lived here before he fled
leaving behind a note that read:

"I'm tired of a God who keeps picking me up and
dropping me."

II. Fragmented Catholicism

Prayer on the Eve of Battle

God of power ███████

███████ love ███████

███████████ to live,

███ to serve ████ to reign.

Through █████████████████████ the archangel,

████████████ in battle against ██████

███ me ████████████ war and violence

██████ establish ██ law ██████ and justice.

Grant this ████████████ Lord.

Pater Noster

Our ▓▓▓▓▓▓ art ▓▓▓▓▓▓

Hallowed b▓ ▓y ▓m▓

▓y Kingdom ▓▓▓

▓▓ Will ▓▓▓▓▓ earth as it is ▓▓▓▓▓ Give us ▓▓▓▓▓▓ bread.

And forgive ▓▓▓▓▓▓

▓▓▓▓▓▓ those who ▓ pass ▓▓▓ us.

▓▓ lead us ▓▓ to tempt▓▓

▓▓▓▓▓▓▓ evil

Prayer to Saint Michael

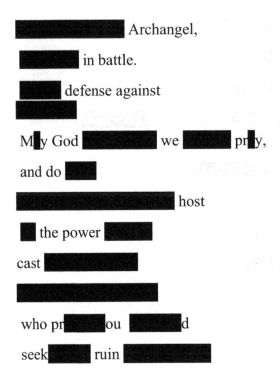 Archangel,

████ in battle.

████ defense against
████

M█y God ████ we ████ pr█y,

and do ███

████████████ host

█ the power ████

cast ██████

██████████

who pr█ █ ou ███ d

seek ███ ruin ██████

Ava Maria

Hail █████

██████████,

The Lord █ ███████

Blessed ████████████ women,

blessed ████ fruit

████ thy womb, █████

█████ M██y,

Mother of ████

████████ sinners ████

████ at the hour of death.

Act of Contrition

O my ███

I am ██████ sorry for

having offended ████

███ I ██ test ██ my sins,

because I dread the loss

█████████ of hell;

███ most of all because

███ offend Thee████████,

Who are all █████████

deserving of all my

████████ resolve,

with ██ help ██████████

to confess ████████

█████████

████████ my life.

The Serenity Prayer

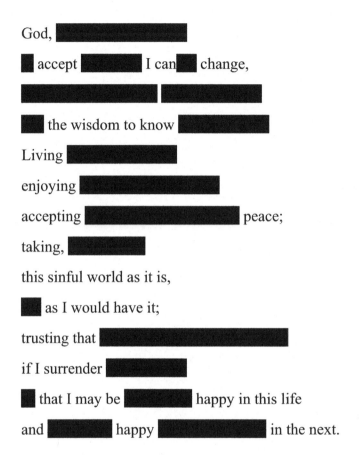

God, ▇▇▇▇▇▇▇▇▇

▇ accept ▇▇▇▇ I can▇ change,

▇▇▇▇▇▇▇▇▇▇▇ ▇▇▇▇▇▇▇

▇ the wisdom to know ▇▇▇▇▇▇

Living ▇▇▇▇▇▇

enjoying ▇▇▇▇▇▇▇▇▇

accepting ▇▇▇▇▇▇▇▇▇ peace;

taking, ▇▇▇▇▇▇

this sinful world as it is,

▇ as I would have it;

trusting that ▇▇▇▇▇▇▇▇▇▇

if I surrender ▇▇▇▇▇

▇ that I may be ▇▇▇▇ happy in this life

and ▇▇▇▇ happy ▇▇▇▇▇▇ in the next.

III. A Tour of Other Lives

Frida and Leon

A child of the revolution
a maker of it
meet amid heat sweltering and tequila sweating
the Mexican sun can set free or burn the European mind

-He Arrives-

Spine straight, old body beaten by The Revolution
the better mannered call his hair steel
he knows it's gray, but says nothing
silence sometimes creates fear which is useful

The raging mind that killed the Tsar
that gave force to Lenin's dream
still puts words to paper
here in Aztec exile

She greets him smiling
her hero since she first donned a red scarf
exotic, clad in a Chiapas dress
vibrant against Adobe, scrub, and cactus

Natalia hates her on sight
she already knows
fire attracts itself
self-immolation takes many forms
-Frida can't sleep-
-Leon can't sleep-

To take your hero as your lover
both pursued, sentenced to death
so take what you can in the dark
For the Revolution
Russian tongue tastes Mexican breast

sex becomes political expression
after Lenin, before Lennon
in another room
Natalia weeps alone
in another
Diego paints murals of his idol

All the while his idol possesses his wife
and is possessed by her
the voice of the proletariat lays moaning
she swallows the revolution in barren womb

-It ends-

As a child
steel pierced her
life unable to grow within
so she gave birth through art
as an old man
steel pierced his skull
and The Revolution oozed from the wound
making a puddle on the floor
crimson on pale
like her face in a painting

*Mexican artist and Communist activist Frida Kahlo and
Communist leader Leon Trotsky engaged in an affair
during his exile in Mexico City. The affair resulted in
he and his wife Natalia leaving the home Frida shared
with her husband, fellow artist and activist Diego
Rivera. His move to a less secure location contributed
to his eventual assassination on the orders of Josef
Stalin.*

Diego

When he was 24, the love of his life was born
with no idea that she had arrived
he continued on the course he had set
brush and palette in hand
the entire world made to be painted
the beginning of the new century
a perfect time to be a muralist
with walls rising across the world
with tequila and cigar in hand
the entire world was made to be laid

Each model though
was far more satisfying in two dimensions
than she was in three
he painted what he saw
while they loved what they wanted to see

All the while she grew
repeatedly colliding with life
she knew he existed
he knew nothing of her
unaware
of the point
where she became the crucified Madonna
sacrificed to the modern gods of steel and progress
impaled upon a sword
forged by the mind of Henry Ford

Upon her resurrection
laid out in the comfort of a middle class tomb
that was a teenage girl's bedroom
she set out to rebuild her soul
crippled but finally picking up speed
catching up to him

Until she walked beside him
her own brush and palette in hand
he was forced
to ask her to slow down
so he could hold her hand

Both by now carrying scars
inflicted by life
hers were more visible
his were more painful
equally broken
they became a whole
around whom
upon whom
others broke themselves
their art post-modern
their love abstract
finding its way onto canvas and plaster
in hues of blue, green, and red
ending where she began
again on a bed
her body broken beyond repair
his broken by age and despair
his body outlived hers
but his art went to the grave with her

*Diego Rivera was a Mexican artist and the husband of
Frida Kahlo. Their lives together, apart, and together
again are works of art the equal of anything they
created.*

Max

Eastman's clock ran long,
starting as a child at Clemens' knee
into a village then; now, only in name,
where Dylan and Cohen pissed on his footsteps

Past the pink early hours
into the red afternoon,
when the seconds ticked by
with the death of
Lenin
Reed
Trotsky
and finally
belief

The atheist heart,
that found God in the masses,
found in the evening that the red flag
merely covered a golden calf

The Austrians showed him
that the gold and not the calf
was what was important
and he followed, always from a distance

The gold should serve man
through Smith's free hand
a lesson only Chicago bound Austrians
could understand

Gold should not be made into a cross
or become the base metal
of bombs burning
verdant green jungles

As his clock struck midnight,
bombs of gold
burned red flags
and he dreamed of The Village.

*Max Eastman was a one-time Bohemian, radical, and
communist who later embraced Neo-Conservatism.
Ever one to follow his conscience, he remained a
lifelong atheist opposed to American military
adventurism and opponent of the evangelical Christian
presence within politics.*

Pablo Neruda: Imperialist, Rapist

Poetry that embraces the political kills the birth of the
  poem
What survives is the stillborn placenta of propaganda

Ask Pablo Neruda,
writhing on his bed;
gripping his gut where plunger pressed poison into the
place below the strong heart that tried to beat until the
end.

Pablo Neruda, ora pro nobis,
did you pray to a red flagged Anubis?
A prayer above the Tamil girl you raped?
A prayer for forgiveness?
Or did you deny the need for prayer like a good
communist?

The liberation theologians have canonized you.
The poets who followed have lionized you.
The feminists of today all claim to despise you.
Pablo Neruda, you brought western soul death in
  Chilean skin;
taking by force what gifts wouldn't buy you.
Only after decades were you made to pay;
thanks to the vagaries of Pinochet.
First your death rattle and in the moments after,
did your dying mind hear the Tamil girl's laughter?

*Pablo Neruda has long been hailed as a poet of genius,
with socialist/communist, anti-imperialist, anti-
colonial, and pro-indigenous views. History is a more
harsh judge than hagiography.*

For Ted Hughes

For Ted Hughes
who made the mistake
of allowing himself
to become the monster
in the myths of others
because of him
Gen X poets
couldn't get dates
due to the warnings
of boomer mothers

Our dear Sylvia
feminist icon
canonized in a cloud of monoxide
rather than incense
only needed someone to fight
needed someone to bite
Ted, where were you that night
she set her own destiny to 350 and baked for eternity
who wants muffins or a soufflé

You Ted walked into this
and willingly became
the most hated man since Hitler
for every female lit major
Born after 1960
as an Englishman
you should have known better
Iron Man rusted
for 40 years

You carried her coffin on your back
blamed for someone else's madness
all while purging your own
onto page after page
holding the hands of the child woman and little man
she left in your care
a jaguar when laden cannot pace at will
a hawk's wings when clipped, make it only a predator
  parrot

Your sin of seeking insanity
punished by the departure
and death of lover and daughter
did you learn then to cease being drawn to madness

You dragged two more coffins behind you
woman and child within
plowing the fields of your farm
turning up the soil with each new attack on you

What drove you to destroy so much
what drove you to find women who wanted to be
  destroyed
why did you agree to be the instrument of their
  destruction

There is no denying your own pathos
learned on English bog and hilltop
no denying the toll it took on your own heart
to the point that even it had enough
and decided to stop

Inside every man is a monster
inside every monster is a man
who can hold and love a woman as a husband
who can hold and love a child as a father

who can call on God in a child's voice
a mimicking mockery of innocence
contained within a poem or a prayer
a supplication and degradation of the soul

Dear God,
you made me in your image
but I did not know you were a surrealist

It was always about the women
each a poem you couldn't put on a page
each a poem you saw begun but could not complete
so each a draft discarded
or from which you were distracted
each even now well regarded
their names in your works redacted

Save for the gassed bookends
the sweet savior whose soul sought destruction that
could be blamed on someone else
and the other who had been running from the gas
chamber since childhood
until she decided to enter it sua sponte

This is now how you're known
the Yorkshire seducer
who left behind ruin
rage
pain
and who stained as many bedsheets
as you did sheets of paper
both are of equal value at auction

*Ted Hughes was a Poet Laureate and a literary giant of
the 20th Century. His marriage to poet Sylvia Plath and
her subsequent suicide is viewed by many in black and
white terms. The whole of their relationship though is
far more complex and tragic. His life following her
death was equally filled with tragedy when his second
wife also committed suicide along with their daughter.
His writing at times almost has the feel of an exorcism.*

Claude

Impression, Soleil Levant
Impression, Sunrise

Binding, blinding, orange early morning star
reduced, controlled, fixed in place in the combination of
red and yellow oils

Bound, round, eternal brushstroke sun
Dead man long gone forever holds oar in water sailing
toward a pier in Le Havre harbor

Claude waited and painted
paints while he waits
for that moment to capture
that will fill the world with rapture
casting aside artistic norms
daring to soften realistic forms
covering the walls of college dorms
his canvases now worth more than his bones
we stare at his work while he lies alone
buried near the water lilies beneath French loam
Clemenceau's shade pulls the black cloth away
the eternal echo of hearing him say
words needed in the dark world today
"Pas de noir pour Monet!"
"No black for Monet!"

*Claude Monet, French Impressionist painter. If you
don't know who he is, talk to a Gen-Xer who went to
college, his paintings adorned the walls of many dorms.*

Cavafy

Cavafy was a Greek boy out of place with a British
  accent
he carved with words a Hellenic space
of an Islamic place
Alexandria will always be more Greek than Arab

Let the Muezzin call the faithful to prayer
let the women hide their faces and cover their hair
let the Imam call for modesty in Mosque or public
  square

It is Alexander's name that fills the air
anytime they are asked, "where is your home"

Cavafy was a Greek voice that spoke in measured Attic
  tones
giving even banal Arabic the beauty of semi-precious
  stones
for his poems though
they were meant for Greek and Greek alone

The Greek learned at the knee of his father by now long
  gone
the Greek that evolved from ancient chorus to bawdy
  sea shanty song
The Greek shared with Hericlea his mother each night
The Greek whispered to his lovers in the demimonde
  each night
The Greek written in neat bureaucratic hand
The Greek that masked the passions of the man
The Greek that ceased to be spoken when the tumors
  took his throat
The Greek from the grave that mocks the moralists and
  continues to gloat

Constantine Cavafy was a Greek poet of the early 20th century who spent almost his entire life living in Alexandria, Egypt. The city and Greek history heavily influenced his poetry. He stands out for being not only a Greek Christian in an Islamic dominated society but also as a gay man who wrote publicly about his sexual orientation.

Thomas

July 27th 1942
Merton the contradiction
stood still
rare for the man
around whom the world turned faster
than it does for you and I
surrounded by Kentucky blue grass
surrounded by the silence of Trappist simplicity
European identity overcome
by Catholicism
surrounded by the remnants of the confederacy
Gethsemani
named for the garden of suffering
the background for a reunion
the brother John Paul
clad in Army green
newly minted lieutenant
bars shining on his shoulders
newly minted Catholic
by faith and Brother Monk's love and instruction
embraced Thomas and strode away
certain in the way of young men
that he would emerge unscathed
from the Europe ablaze
he would add to those flames
raining bombs down upon
cities where Thomas had once stayed
until he fell from the sky one day
metal birds are funny that way
resting now somewhere beneath the channel
the sea that divided Thomas from the land
where he had been a child
and the land where he became child-man before
continuing his pilgrimage west

After his brother John Paul Daedalus fell from the sky
Thomas set about asking the silent why
a heart turned against war long before
felt his resistance to it grow even more
in Gethsemani where once marched blue and gray
the insistent why wouldn't go away
each time he stood and looked to the East
mourning man for rejecting peace
Thomas the contemplative walked the halls
Thomas the anarchist behind the walls
Thomas the pacifist could hear the calls
of those who had read his words and wanted more

It would be 20 years of writing words that reached
millions of minds
it would be 20 years before he would find
the opportunity to pass through Gethsemani's gate
to venture out into the nuclear world of hate
in that the demonic year of 1968

Thomas met with men of peace
the Buddhists and Hindus joined the priest
En Persona Christi he arrived in Thailand
offering all a brother's hand
until he was found on the floor near his bed
blood curiously pouring from his head
the Bishop ensured his body was blessed
before they removed the Hitachi fan from across his
  chest
loaded into a C-5 instead of a tomb
the dead GIs happy to make room
the man who mourned their waste in war
strapped down beside them on aluminum floor
the plane flew east taking him to Gethsemani
as he flew like his brother over the sea

Thomas Merton was a Trappist monk, activist, poet, writer, mystic, and thinker. His autobiography, The Seven Storey Mountain, written in 1948, stands as one of the most powerful conversion stories written in the 20th Century. He died under mysterious circumstances in Thailand in 1968.

Hulme's Elegy

Where is Hulme?
The imagist reduced to the meat of the matter
the meat that was matter
meat that didn't matter
meat is matter
murdered matter
murder doesn't matter
when a generation dies
for King and Country

Hulme is gone
deconstructed like a poem to the basics
an atomized mist
spread along the trenches
without form or structure

Hulme is gone
what was left
wouldn't fill Williams' Red Wheelbarrow
wouldn't make a stanza in Pound's Cantos
wouldn't be noticed by Eliot's Prufrock
wouldn't be worthy of a glance from H.D.'s Helen

Hulme is gone
his entire existence obliterated,
reduced to a crater courtesy of the Kaiser who had no
  use for art or poetry
Wagner's discordant brass crescendo drowned out by
the whistle of an incoming artillery round

Hulme is gone
he left behind memories perhaps
but even those are gone
the people who held those memories are dead too
those women he loved
remembered the dead man
whose touch and thrust gave ecstasy
shivered when the felt his ghost pass
until they joined him

Hulme is gone

War kills the poet
kills poetry
words aren't enough
even a century later

*T.E. Hulme's poetry influenced the Imagist/Modernist
Movement. He was killed on the Western Front during
World War I*

IV. Pieces of War

Poetry at War

Fake poetry
is mistaken often
for the real thing
as the language of love
misconstrued
as written from a place of weakness

The poet seen
as effete
effeminate
sprawled on a chaise
passing the days in pursuit
of women he cannot have

That is not poetry
that is how cowards hide
as they've done from war to war
demanding better men give more and more
secured by stronger men while in safety they reside

Cowards write
bloodless sonnets and cri du couer
works best read within Parisian sewers

Cowards write triumphant odes and scores
in Vichyesque obeisance to conquering Teutonic or
Islamist hordes

Cowards write to curry favor
with culture's prevailing winds
read their intersectional works on transgendered Lemur
  feminism

Cowards write to create the world they seek
where to be a man, one must be weak
Cowards write hidden and out of sight
when they hear Hemingway is looking for a fight

This is not poetry

Poetry is war
emotion and story
concentrated into lines
marching stanzas
forms are Katas
practiced with all the devotion
of a written martial religion

Poetry is discipline
a legionnaire
who has marched
from Gaul to Germania
who has spent so long
fighting for Rome
that he is no longer Roman
no longer has a home
he has become a barbarian
to defend civilization

Poetry is violence
Elegant slashes across the page
thrust, parry, riposte, with fine point blade
Mayakovsky adopted the Russian weapon of sharpened
  spade
The battlefield and bookstore are universities
where survival is your passing grade

Where is the poet while the imposter writes?
Here is the Poet
words are weapons
honed to the same sharpened edge as a saber
aimed with the same lethal accuracy
as Hathcock's rifle

The poet
can kill from a distance
the target unaware
until line or stanza
plunges into the mind
the bright white flash of impact
leaving behind the shimmering pink halo
of headshot and understanding
both are fatal

Before the War

I was a Soldier
who had become a sailor
adrift on becalmed waters
no shore visible in any direction
A rusted in place rudder
my compass pawned long ago
at some port or other
numbed to a present no different from the past
a future as unconcerned with me as I was with it

The boat leaked but its cracks were sealed
by scotch and sarcasm
and the refusal to admit to
each shoal or sandbar
where I had run aground
I was never a good sailor

At some point
I switched the naval ensign
for the Jolly Roger
But before long
I flew no flag at all
unsure of where to place my loyalty
other than to the current
that decided where I would go

One wine weary morning
made bleary by dawn and sunlight
the feeling of something off
something not right

From the deck I watched four hawks fly overhead
in the direction of my future
they collided with it
setting the world around me on fire
burning off the rust
rekindling old embers in my heart

Setting a course was easy
pointing the bow in the direction
of smoke and conflagration
that I could see on the horizon
a cloud by day
a pillar of fire by night

Following backward
the path of the hawks
a back azimuth into history
Alexander proved to be
the greatest navigator
thanks to Arrian
and a worn copy of the Odyssey
translated by Lawrence
they provided comfort on those nights
where the creak of wood
sounded like the screeching of hawks

I landed on a strange shore
setting out to scale mountains
to find the crags, cliffs, and crevices
where hawks were known to dwell

I found my way to a nest
I smashed the eggs
and killed all the hawks I could find
lest they too fly into the mountains
my children had built of their futures

Now others gather around me
and I teach them how to hunt the hawks
how to destroy
how to bring fire
how to burn the nests to ash

The first lesson:
when your ship touches land
burn it
then you have no choice
but to hunt

Cold War Poem 1979

The baked potatoes at Ponderosa
are wrapped in foil
awaiting their consumption
drowned in sour cream, bacon, bits, scallions, and
always the butter
as the greatest generation feasts on the fruits of their
labor having vanquished Hitler and Hirohito having
spawned the boomers who spread like locusts
singing a Vietnamese opera droning I Me My

The rewards for victory include colon and prostate
  cancer
the foil wrapped potato and recooked charred steak
providing carcinogens beyond counting

A cheap meal of the Pax Americana is a gauntlet
thrown down in Cold War posturing
The TV revealing (after slapping it on the side to
improve the picture)
a Babushka waiting in line for a loaf of black bread
that will be washed down with vodka by Diedushka
who wonders what he won in the Great Patriotic War

We won the Cold War
and Ponderosa closed

War Poem

To write poems of ruin
black ink bears the memory of shadow and smoke
the hearth is cold
sounds echo on vacant stone

Fathers march in lockstep
for what do they fight?
Pro patria?
Pro familia?
Pro Dei?
mothers huddled with sons and daughters
counting sunsets and moons

It was the 35th sunset and the 2-quarter moon when he
  departed
the message arrived on a new moon
and the masons at once set to work on the epitaph
the infant suckling mother's breast tasted tears for the
  first time
and learned its first lesson

Gold Star

The illusion of ease
Trapped beneath tectonic memory
Of garters and stockings
Worn in anticipation
Of a victorious nation
And the return of her man

Daily staring through the window
Until the arrival of the telegram
And the garters get put away
And forgotten

Cedar and moth ball sodden
Discovered decades later
Next to a black and white photo
Of a defined leg and derriere
Held by a hand
Now bone in some no-man's land
Still clutching a rifle

Captain Ahad

I sat next to the Captain, a veteran of the Soviet and
Civil Wars, drinking a lukewarm cup of chai.

The expanse of his forehead and crown brown and
lined, like a paper bag that has been used, folded,
reused and folded again.
His beard black and lustrous, save for the scar down the
left side of his face, a river of puckered flesh.
His eyes were opal pits, reduced to slits, from years of
looking through a gun sight beneath the Afghan sun.

Time is measured in cups of chai, not in the sweep of
the watch hands, so it is two and a half cups of chai that
pass before we speak.
I ask, "Commandant Sayed, Jig-Tooran, Abdul-Jan,
what will you do when the war is over?"
He smiles, shrugs and says, "Wait for the next one."

The Smells

I remember them at the strangest times
burning tires ever present
a latrine made for westerners,
the holes in the floor a concession to local custom
smog, sand, that cold smell that warned of winter
matched by the creep of snow down the caps of the
Takur Ghar

Sweat dried permeating clothing
the smell of a room full of Afghans
for whom bathing was a luxury

The good ones-
my pipe tobacco
cigars
naan baking
CLP on newly cleaned weapons
the inside of a box from home
the shirt I asked my wife to wear and then send me
on my pillow a comforting scent as I drifted off to sleep
7,000 miles from all that was familiar

I miss those smells

People Always Want to Know About Afghanistan

I am the actor
in the movie everyone remembers
No matter what else he's done
typecast into a role
it was one year of my life
one year out of more than 40
all the other things I've been
escape your notice

What do you want to know?
What should I tell you?
Why should I tell you?
Of boredom punctuated by the occasional rocket?
Fear in the valley on the Bagram road?
The constant searching
for the evil white corolla
ubiquitous?
The Flying Dutchman, the White Whale of Afghanistan
The smells, sounds, sights, tastes?

You wouldn't understand or care
They can't be recreated or described
no matter how good an Afghan restaurant you've
   found
Of import to you, the future
Can it survive, thrive, (your pet issue here), are we
winning?
Of import to me, the past and the now
How are the Askari I trained and lived with?
Are my terps safe?
You speak as an expert on Sunday shows
You lecture me on the latest article
   interview

107

white paper
news story
yet you don't even know
They are Afghans, not Afghani.
You ask me if I speak the language?
I ask which one?
I greet you in Dari
You think I am fluent

You want war stories?
I have none to give you
I have humor and mirth
I tell you anyway
You started this conversation
and I will give you what you asked for
much to your chagrin

The stories of stolen olive oil
of coke straw and snaggle tooth
of the one who cracked the code
of tres leche
of maddening pubic hair on urinals
of working for the Dept. of Agriculture
of ___ Chicken
of cigars and profanity
pipe tobacco with Canadians
Albanian auto maintenance
frozen fuel lines
chess with a savant

You look bored I apologize
Clearly I am not who you thought I'd be
You might be surprised to know
I'm not who I thought I'd be either
I am not a hero I am a Seanchai

108

But the tales I tell
are understood only by those who were there.

Would you like to hear of the other 39 years?
Of my daughters, my sons, my wife?
Of their pain and sacrifice due to my absence?
Apparently not nice chatting
People always want to know about Afghanistan...

Indirect Fire

In the darkness where the siren howls
we leapt at the beginning of its grinding growl
we laughed as we dove beneath our cots
as steel of Chinese rockets plunged into nearby spots

Orgasmic elation followed
as shrapnel fell in a torrent of rusted hail
"He's got the distance measured"
said one soul in the darkness
our tent was torn like Nelson's sail

The sexy British siren's voice told us all was clear
and maybe it was but we still felt fear
We laughed in the way the condemned laugh at the
  gallows
a madman's laugh that is loud yet hollow

That fear didn't dissipate or fade that day
to be honest I think it never will go away
When a siren screams in the dark I throw myself to the
  floor
and a confused American woman's voice asks,
"What did you do that for?"

Which is why I sit with this pistol on the bed
trying to silence the siren in my head
Into the storm with shredded sail I steer
and I smile wishing I could hear
the British siren's voice tell me all is clear

Veterans Day

Today brought to you by
thank you for your service
I barely notice it anymore
when it's said
unless it's a child
who sees the uniform
and dreams of being me

Dream different dreams child
dream of freedom and peace
dream of sleeping in
dream of Moleskine notebooks
dream of passion and pastries
dream of steaks and Cabernet
dream of good cheese
dream of vacations
dream of books that you will have time to read
dream of traveling to places
where no one is shooting at you
and the hotel has a nice view
of the streets and skyline
so you can watch happy well fed people
go about their lives

Those are things you want
when you are me
when you feel
duty and responsibility
wrap their arms around you
holding you in place
while another day passes
until they all have passed
and there is no time
left to dream

That which is permitted to others
is forbidden unto thee
even a day of freedom
where I am allowed to just be me

Tommy Visits Valhalla

Heaven and hell are booming
but Valhalla ain't what it used to be
the spineless and the cowards all prefer
an eternal certainty

A place where they can roam or roast to their hearts
  content
where everything's decided
they eschew the longhouse for the revival tent
where scriptural salvation is provided

While here I sit with comrades of my battles
and those fought long before
free from sanctimonious faddle,
biblical interpretation, and evangelizing boors

I have always had more in common
with the foe who stood to fight against me
than I do with the citizen who calls for action
with no thought given to my mortality

There are no refreshing springs
the Valkyries serve only beer
you'd hate the songs we sing
and know you ain't welcome here

For this is a place of peace
only to those who have known war
the Imam, Rabbi, and the Priest wouldn't be allowed
'cross the threshold
not one foot on the floor

We listened to your absolution, prayers and prattle
your demand that we choose the path that's straight
the same words recited before every battle,
but not before you passed the collection plate

Heaven has no desire for our parties
that will always go beyond the dawn
hell fears our drunken sorties
worried that we would stay too long

We found ourselves disappointed
by the lack of people when we arrived
realizing that the martyrs and the holy anointed
never really wanted to survive

So we who here are gathered
celebrate but always watch the door
knowing that the time here doesn't matter
you'll always need us for another war

Memorial Day Fishing Trip

Standing amidst green and silence
wooded meditation
sound of frogs plunging into water
the flick and turn of cast and reel
waiting for the inevitable pull and vibration on rod

Alone
even the mind quiet

But still

Listening for the sounds of threat
the click of the reel
is the selector switch moving from safe to semi
the twang of the line pulled from a hooked bush
is the tripwire being broken

The swish of the rod from side to side mimics my eyes
sweeping left right
a ripple in the water
draws my eye
and I bring the rod up
In line with the target
I can hit the center of the ripple with the line
30 feet out
my brain still computes distance and engagement
like I am holding a rifle
and not a rod

Pull the fish from the water
its eyes bulging as it flops about in the grass
and the poor bastard
who tried to plant the IED
But they forgot to put handle with care in Pashto

(not that he could read)
is flopping around on the ground
grasping and gasping
trying to literally pull himself together

He was too small to keep
so throw him back

I wonder if dementia will be a blessing in my old age
making it so that I don't have to remember
and can fish without knowing what I've already caught

The Clearing Barrel

1. Approach the barrel, visually inspect your weapon, and ensure the weapon is on safe.

When you meet new people outside of your world
use caution
they're not likely to understand you
they'll be made uncomfortable
if they know what you are
even when you mean no harm
you are still capable of it
that counts against you
in the normal world
don't talk about what you've seen
don't talk about what you've done
don't leave an opening that allows them
to see that you're on safe

2. Point the muzzle of the weapon into the barrel. Maintaining control of both, remove the magazine from the weapon.

The most visible dangerous part of you
should be the first thing you do away with
Put your blade into your pocket so its clip isn't visible
the skeleton holster
fits under your shirt
grow your hair
drink to diminish your SA

Don't ask those questions you asked
when you came into a village
don't look for the exits
don't look up at rooftops
when going into and out of buildings
don't sweep left/right when driving
use your peripheral vision instead
learn how to make small talk
laugh when everyone else does
avoid the hyenas and the coyotes
you will lose any fight with them
even if you win
especially if you win

3. Keeping the muzzle pointed into the barrel, eject the live round from the chamber.

This the part of you
that can do the most damage
the round always ready to fire
without it
you are at your most vulnerable
defenseless
that round has been your lifeline
without it,
you have to fight fair
without it
you give your opponent a chance
you know
that's not how war works
you should have every advantage
they should have none
that is how you win
now the odds are even

4. Keeping the weapon pointed into the barrel, turn the selector switch from safe to fire and pull the trigger

-click-
The sound of impotence
a message to the world
that you are harmless
this is the one thing
you don't want
the world to know
for the longest time
you sought to convey
the exact opposite
it kept others at a distance
it kept you immune
from the fate that befell the less fortunate
the less well armed
it kept you safe
It kept you alive

5. Return the weapon to safe and place it in the holster, secure your live round in the magazine, insert the magazine into your ammo pouch, you are now cleared to enter your facility

You can now go home
but you can't fight

119

The Centurion's Lot

To carry sword, shield, and spear
to fight
for a Republic
then an Empire

To gather around a fire each night
far from those in whose name you fight

Winning submission
but submitting your will
your hopes, dreams, desires
your daughters become women
your sons struggle to be men
both without your hand on their shoulder
your hands are too callused to touch them anyway
you only cause pain

Your reward
is a grave in a place not your own
and the hope that another sword will carry your
  memory
because what you are
is politics by other means

Night Terrors

I'm ending my own life
there is a pistol in my hand
another hand grips mine
"Let go of my fucking hand"
I wake up gripping my own wrist

Homecoming

The first night home you're standing on the beach just
at the place where the water, still cold, wraps alkaline
foam about your feet threatening to pull you down and
in, like your Uncle did in summer when you were
standing at pool's edge. You were afraid of things then.
There were still monsters. It was a lovely time to be
alive.

The sand beneath you is familiar but its feel is not, this
is smooth sand, peaceful sand, first world sand that
doesn't know war, famine, or death. This sand doesn't
know anything about radical Islam. It asks you
questions of its distant relatives, the sands where you
were that had never seen the ocean, it wants to
understand, but you don't want to explain. You're tired
of the stares filled with inappropriate questions.
You grind your heel into the sand until it understands
and grows silent.

The wind doesn't ask questions, it just blows strong
from the east, trying to collect the pieces of you that
you left behind and pushing them across the ocean back
to you. The wind though, is a leaky bucket and what
you'd left back of yourself is again dropped along the
way residing where you left it in Hohenfels, in Tirana,
in Kandahar, in Kabul, in Mazar-e-Sharif, in Ghazni, in
Tangy Kalay, in places that don't have names, only 10
digit grids. Having nothing to return, the wind just
wraps around you welcoming.

The moon is full, a small second sun that is an ally well
known to you after staring at its cracks and lines from
atop mountains 7,000 miles away from where you now
stand; you're a different person beneath the same moon.

122

The moon, having the divine right of queens, of being a fan of Divine in Hairspray and Pink Flamingos, asserts her right to speak:

"You have returned from whence you came. This is not home and the illusion of that has been dispelled. You know that home is a place you do not know. You see that all here is the same but you have changed. It wasn't your war. You were too much a coward to fight your war, but no longer."

With that everything around me becomes numb and normal again
I want a drink

For Joe

Seven years since you came home on your shield and a
Spartan mother wept

I went to where you had fallen to seek a reckoning
and found only frustration
no one would come out to do battle
to claim the honor for your kill
to face me claiming my due
my spear remained dry

I returned angry
at a people who wouldn't face me
who had killed you without the fortitude to face you
at myself for not living up to my own demands
at our own people
grown soft on the harvest watered by your blood
uncaring
unknowing
bland platitudes and passive lip service
of gratitude for debt they cannot comprehend
I miss you brother

My son carries your name
you should see him
he will know you
and in peace will live to be worthy of your sacrifice

Soon my own shield, sword, and spear will be laid
  down
and you will be spoken of in the memories of an old
  man

and in each telling you will grow more heroic
until one day the story will be worthy
of the man you were

Rest in Peace and know you are not forgotten
as I carry your memory around the walls of Troy.

1LT Joseph Theinert was killed in action on 04Jun2010

Cognitive Behavior Therapy

Walk the middle path she says
so you do
Scanning both sides of the road
for trash and culverts where IEDs can be hidden
looking for ant trails where command wires are buried
you dismount from the safety of your truck
performing your 0-5-25 checks
scanning-------------!

"Are you having a flashback right now?"

You're in her office
that's carpet under your feet
not dirt.
Your hands gripping the arms of the couch.
How do you tell her that even on the middle path,
you still worry about being blown up?

Afterword

Defining the self
The Poet is the midwife
The Poem is the placenta of memory

Anthony Roberts is a poet, educator, and veteran. A graduate of The New School in New York City with a Master of Fine Arts degree, he has taught at Fairleigh Dickinson University and Seton Hall University. His poetry has been published in Southerly Literary Journal, The Other Voices Poetry Anthology, and Vox Poetica among others and has been translated into Persian, Italian, Bengali and Czech. His first book, Pigtown, was published in 2017 by Red Dashboard Publications and was selected by Old Dominion University for inclusion in their writing program.

He currently lives in Hunterdon County, NJ in a home with beautiful views and interlocking fields of fire.

63626546R00080